NATURE

Why Do We Need SOIL?

by Laura K. Murray

PEBBLE
a capstone imprint

Published by Pebble, an imprint of Capstone
1710 Roe Crest Drive, North Mankato, Minnesota 56003
capstonepub.com

Library of Congress Cataloging-in-Publication Data is available on the Library of Congress website.

ISBN: 9780756575274 (hardcover)
ISBN: 9780756575229 (paperback)
ISBN: 9780756575236 (ebook PDF)

Summary: What's so great about soil? A lot, actually! In this Pebble Explore book, discover how this often overlooked—or even annoying—part of nature is essential to our world. We need soil to grow crops and construct buildings and roads. Soil is even important to the air we breathe.

Editorial Credits
Editor: Donald Lemke; Designer: Sarah Bennett; Media Researcher: Svetlana Zhurkin; Production Specialist: Katy LaVigne

Image Credits
Getty Images: Claudiad, 28, Martin Harvey, 23; Shutterstock: assistant, 10, BlueSnap, 8, Burjan Zsolt (soil background), cover, back cover, and throughout, Faith Forrest (dotted background), cover and throughout, Filip PhotoStock, 20, FlareArts, 24, galitsin, 29 (bottom), golf bress, 13, Igor Stramy, cover, ingehogenbijl, 27, lv-olga, 12, J.J. Gouin, 22, JaneHYork, 21, Jasmine Sahin, 29 (middle), Jitlada Panwiset, 11, K.Decha, 5, Lidiane Miotto, 15, mailsonpignata, 14, Maples Images, 29 (top), markara, 9, neenawat khenyothaa, 19, New Africa, 4, oticki, 25, Pavlo Baliukh, 16, Smileus, 18, snapgalleria, 7, VectorMine, 17

Printed and bound in the USA. 5425

Table of Contents

Words in **bold** are in the glossary.

Help Underfoot

A garden is wet from rain. Now the sun shines bright. The ground begins to dry. Tomatoes hang from vines. Carrots grow underground. Soil holds the plants in place. The soil lets the plants get **nutrients**, air, and water.

Humans, plants, and animals
need soil. Soil helps plants and food
grow. It does a lot more too! Soil is an
important part of nature.

All About Soil

Soil makes up the top layer of the earth. It is full of tiny living things. Soil has been forming for many years. It may take more than 500 years to form one inch (2.5 centimeters) of soil!

Earth's soil is made up of layers. Topsoil is the top layer. Subsoil lies below that. Next comes a layer of broken rock. At the bottom is a solid layer of rock called bedrock.

Did You Know?
The study of soil is called *pedology*.

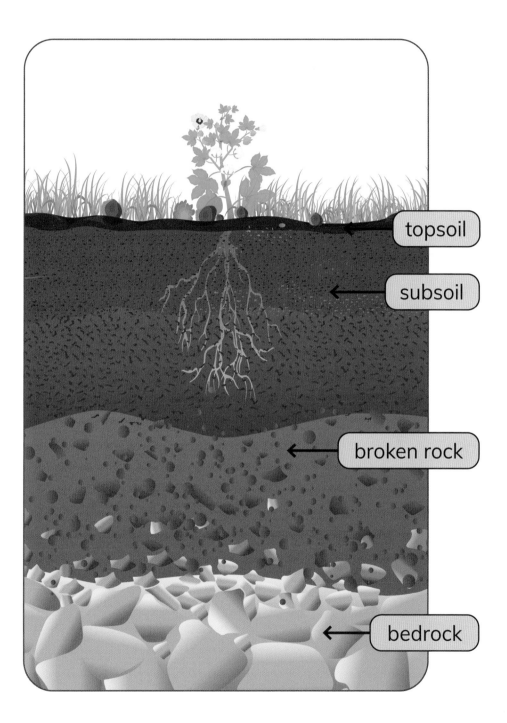

topsoil

subsoil

broken rock

bedrock

Soil forms when rocks and **minerals** break down over time. Wind and rain help break them into tiny bits. Heat and cold help too. The bits mix with rotting plants and animals that have died. Water and air also make up soil.

earthworms

Soil has open spaces called pores. The pores hold air, water, roots, worms, and tiny living things. Healthy soils have many pores of different sizes. They let water, air, and nutrients move through the soil.

There are three main kinds of soil particles. Sand is the largest. Each grain of sand is just 0.002 to 0.08 inches (0.05–2 millimeters). Silt is medium-sized. Clay is the smallest. Particles of silt and clay are too small for the human eye to see.

grains of sand

Soils have different amounts of
sand, silt, and clay. This changes how
the soil feels and acts. For example,
sand feels gritty. Water drains through
it quickly. Clay holds water longer. It
feels sticky when wet.

Just one spoonful of soil has millions of tiny living things! Bugs, slugs, and earthworms make their home in the soil. Bigger animals such as moles and gophers live there too.

gopher

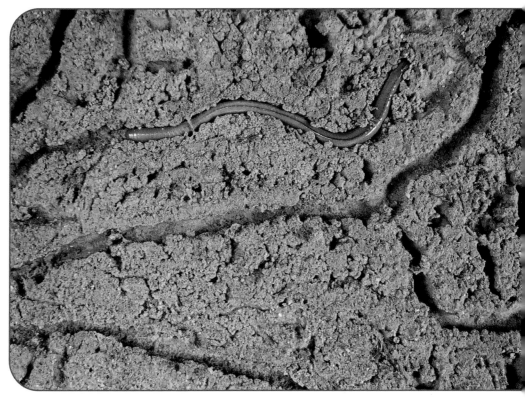
An earthworm creates tunnels in soil.

Earthworms burrow into the ground. This helps air pass through the soil. The earthworms also leave behind waste. The waste is sticky and that keeps the soil together.

How Does Soil Help Us?

Nearly all plants that make food need soil to grow. People use soil to grow fruits and vegetables. They grow corn, wheat, and other crops. Both humans and animals eat food grown in soil.

Corn grows in soil.

roots

Soil gives plants the water, air, and food they need. The soil also gives plant roots a place to grow. The soil holds the plants in place. It protects them from bad weather. Plants in healthy soil can stay strong against sickness and pests.

Healthy soil keeps land from flooding. It lets water pass through instead of running off. Healthy soil helps in dry times too. Plant roots can move deeper to reach water.

Soil also cleans and filters water. When it rains, water travels down through the soil. The soil takes out harmful materials. Helpful **bacteria** and other tiny living things clean the water. Dirty parts get trapped in the soil. Then the clean water moves on.

Soil stores **carbon**. Carbon is a main part of all life on Earth. Most carbon is stored in the oceans. The soil has the most carbon on land.

Carbon can mix with air to make a gas that traps heat. Having too much in the air can make temperatures rise. Soil has an important job in storing carbon. It may help slow **climate change**.

Humans need soil for making buildings, roads, and bridges. People make soil maps before they build. The maps show information about the land and water.

The soil's plants, minerals, and living things help make medicines. They are part of sunscreen, makeup, and other products. Concrete, bricks, and other building materials use parts from soil.

Threats to Soil

Earth's soil is being destroyed faster than it can form. The biggest threat to soil is **erosion**. This is when the top layer of soil is worn down and moved over time.

Wind and rain cause erosion. Humans can cause soil to wear down faster too. They cut down forests. Sometimes farmers let too many animals graze. The soil wears down quickly without as many plants.

Sometimes people do not take care of the land. The soil cannot drain as it should. Farmers may use too much salt when they water crops. Too much salt can destroy the soil. People also harm soil when they cover the land to build on it.

Some farmers spray **fertilizers**, **pesticides**, and other chemicals on crops. Using too many chemicals can kill important things in the soil. It destroys nutrients plants need.

A farmer sprays a field of soybeans with pesticides.

A World Without Soil

Can you imagine a world without soil? Life would not be possible.

The animals and tiny living things in the soil would not exist. Many plants and food crops would not grow. People would not have clothing, medicine, and other products made from the soil. They would have to find new ways to build.

Did You Know?
Soil can be found almost anywhere on Earth, from the top of mountains to the bottom of the ocean.

There would be no land to clean
and filter water. Floods and **droughts**
would be big problems. The planet's
temperatures would shoot up.

It can be easy to forget how important soil is. But soil is an amazing part of nature. Just one scoop is full of life! Humans, plants, and animals need soil to survive.

COOL FACTS ABOUT SOIL

- Soil scientists use science and math to study soil. They may work in wetlands, farming, water research, or many other areas.

- Every state and territory in the United States has a state soil.

- In one acre (0.4 hectares) of soil, the top six inches (15.2 cm) has 20,000 pounds (9,072 kilograms) of living matter.

- Composting is when people recycle food and plant materials to make a natural fertilizer.

- 95 percent of food production needs soil.

- There are approximately 1,400,000 earthworms in one acre (0.4 ha) of cropland.

Glossary

bacteria (bak-TEER-ee-uh)—very small living things that exist everywhere in nature

carbon (KAHR-buhn)—chemical element, found in all living things, that is the basis for life

climate change (KLY-muht CHAYNJ)—a significant change in Earth's climate over a period of time

drought (DROUT)—a long period of weather with little or no rainfall

erosion (i-ROH-zhuhn)—the wearing away of land by water or wind

fertilizer (FUHR-tuh-ly-zuhr)—a substance used to make crops grow better

mineral (MIN-ur-uhl)—a material found in nature that is not an animal or a plant

nutrient (NOO-tree-uhnt)—a substance needed by a living thing to stay healthy

pesticide (PESS-tuh-syde)—a substance used to destroy pests

Read More

James, Emily. *The Simple Science of Dirt*. North Mankato, MN: Capstone, 2018.

Rake, Jody S. *Soil, Silt, and Sand: Layers of the Underground*. North Mankato, MN: Capstone, 2016.

Sipperley, Keli. *Soil*. North Mankato, MN: Capstone, 2021.

Internet Sites

Kids Discover: The Dirt on Soil
kidsdiscover.com/teacherresources/dirt-soil/

Soil Science Society of America: What Is Soil
soils4kids.org/about

Soil Science Society of America: State Soils
soils4teachers.org/state-soils/

Index

About the Author

Laura K. Murray is a Minnesota-based author of more than 100 published or forthcoming books for young readers. She loves learning from fellow readers and helping others find their reading superpowers! Visit her at LauraKMurray.com.